# PENTATEUCH

# WHIT GRIFFIN

# PENTATEUCH

# THE FIRST FIVE BOOKS

SKYSILL PRESS

**ACKNOWLEDGEMENTS**

The author gratefully acknowledges the following editors & publishers:

Eric Elshtain, Beard of Bees; Amanda Schapel, Brooklyn Review; Matthew Henriksen, Cannibal; Amber Nelson, cold-drill; Lee Chapman, First Intensity; Matt Hart & Eric Appleby, Forklift, Ohio; John Phillips, Hassle; Tom Meyer, Jargon Society; Bob Arnold, Longhouse; Michael Whalen & Ed Go, Other Rooms Press; Chris Salerno & Chris Tonelli, Raleigh Quarterly; Dr. Wolfgang Görtschacher & David Miller, Poetry Salzburg Review; Rob MacDonald, Sixth Finch; Andrew Hughes (GMB), The New Left; Michael Schiavo (GMB), The Equalizer; Joe Robitaille, They Are Flying Planes; Arielle Guy, Turntable + Blue Light.

And to my early readers:

Lou Asekoff, Crystal Brandt, Lisa Jarnot, Evan Kennedy (GMB), Jason Myers (GMB), Abdellah Taïa, Chris Zubryd, & others unmentioned.

Thanks also to Sam Ward, for Vision.

Copyright © Whit Griffin 2010
The right of Whit Griffin to be identified as the author has been asserted by him in accordance with Section 77 of the Copyrights, Designs and Patents Act 1988. All rights reserved.
Cover illustration © Adam McLean.

Skysill Press
3 Gervase Gardens
Clifton Village
Nottingham, NG11 8LZ
skysillpress.blogspot.com

# CONTENTS

**MINOR PROPHETS**

| | |
|---|---|
| Whistled Off The Fist | 2 |
| The Need-Fire | 3 |
| Of A Country Garden | 4 |
| Agates In The Badlands | 5 |
| Let The Line Be Restored | 6 |
| To Hear And Obey | 7 |
| From The Common Loon To The Varied Thrush | 8 |
| The Hand Of Glory | 9 |
| The Great Mondard | 10 |
| His Eyes Were Delighted | 11 |
| Borne On Slender Wing | 12 |
| Those Intriguing Nightshades | 13 |
| Mystagogue | 14 |
| An Uncertain Trumpet | 15 |
| Sewn For Ceremony | 16 |
| The Refrain First | 17 |
| Throwing The Fool | 18 |
| The Secret Fire, Traveler's Ease | 19 |

**SUSPICIOUS MINDS**

| | |
|---|---|
| Bright Cup, Burnished Fighter | 22 |
| Ornithomancy | 23 |
| Perdita Peregrination | 24 |
| Special Rider | 25 |
| Commodious Harbour In An Unhealthy Climate | 26 |
| Crawl Space | 27 |
| Greased For The Channel | 28 |
| Lads, Back On The Horse | 29 |
| All One Word | 30 |
| Co. Aytch | 31 |

Early Snowball                                            32
Do This To Remove The Necessity                           33
Armor Of Water                                            34

**SOLOMON'S SEAL**

The October Horse                                         36
Promise Of Noon                                           37
Sacred But Fatal                                          38
As A Swarm Of Bees To A Brass Pan                         39
All Saints                                                40
Acknowldge The Corn                                       41
Movement In The White Mist                                42
Shadow Light                                              43
The Whispering Campaign                                   44
Carry The Bell Away                                       45

**WANHOPE**

All Joining Joyous And Mournful                           48
That's Not Peru                                           49
Commissary Safe                                           51
Spreading Without Let Or Hindrance                        52
Between The House And The Holly Tree                      54
Wanhope                                                   55

**GOLDEN DAWN**

Jacquerie                                                 58
The Question Is Lost                                      59
Sorry Don't Feed The Bulldog                              60
The Banishing Ritual                                      62
Transplanting Nymphaea                                    63

| | |
|---|---|
| Cut From The Bolt This Secret | 64 |
| A Sheaf Of Bearing Arrows | 65 |
| Split The Stick, You Will Find Me There | 66 |
| Day Is Done | 67 |
| The Spirit Of The Staircase | 69 |
| Chimera | 71 |
| A Rightness Of Its Own | 72 |
| Hell For Leather | 73 |
| Inkeeper Grow The Pie | 74 |
| Fireless Wine | 75 |
| Palingenesis | 77 |

# MINOR PROPHETS

# Whistled Off The Fist

Future generations will build prisons
to house men whose crimes have yet
to be invented. For this reason and
more, it's quaint to meet a chimney
sweep, a child with rickets.

A walk through the artillery garden
seldom yields mystical fruit. One
is likely to get lost in a wilderness
of expectation. A common archer can
teach the maestro to draw a straight line.

Summer brings the need to bone
up on Elgar. Egrets convey a grace
that transcends the swamps they call
home. A man doesn't need an ivy
branch to know where wine is sold.

The key is to keep what's moving; the
possibilities are more limited, but the
need to take inventory increases. To
find that one farmer with a spare carpet
and an extra cow. As the Mayans said,
the visible sun is not the real one.

## The Need-Fire

There are those for whom the land
itself is an oracle. Those who know
what miracles the ground may bestow.
Root systems remember the soil
from which they were removed. The
fresh leaves of parsley prevent miscarriage,
the dried seeds induce abortion. Magpies
have carried these seeds to improbable
places. The Romans petitioned Robigus
to protect the wheat from mildew.
Rain collected from a violent storm
will impart those properties on to the
one who drinks it. You don't have to
agree with the concepts to make use of
the energy they create.

## Of A Country Garden

To combat the old empire's new
problems, an attention span is required
that will focus farther than a fresh shave.
There's an impatience to the impermanence.

Jays fight over the right to bathe
in the fountain, even in the rain. May
you always be allowed to live according
to your nature. May your melancholy
tend toward the softer end.

Think Albinoni and oarsmen, summer
salads of borage flowers and rocket.
Canapés on the portico, admiring the
cupressus. The conversion may take
hold even as the fish course is being served.
The nubile and the willing always have an easier go.

## Agates In The Badlands

Storms sweep across the prairie,
the boxwork cave exhales. Leek
as lightning rod, a tincture of arnica
will remedy a dog's fear of thunder.
Brittle plants become supple as the
full moon approaches. Gather bracken
when a comet is in the sky.

In the small hours, no one could be
persuaded to cross a natural bridge.
The note has been secured. The story
remains true. Virgins have no reason
to mutiny. Magnolias are seldom
treated to Caruso. Most carp will
never taste Montrachet.

Some identify colors by touch. That
Clio's scroll may touch our modest
mountain. Keep calm and carry on.
Martens have a weakness for mistletoe,
the witches' broom. To practice self-
restraint at buffet and bridge toll. To
see plainly without a pair of spectacles.

It's not tobacco, but it's also not
chestnut tree. The feet are standard
in all methods, the arms have their
own positions. Ask Cecchetti. The
moon is mutable to some, permanent
to others. The bountiful table, a
testament to rain.

## Let The Line Be Restored

Spring in the crosshairs, winter's
ice played hell with the hardwoods.
Here in Beulah Land, the Florida
Cracker is making a comeback. A
friend has found a physician who
makes house calls.

Men of pen and inkhorn carefully
measure the moon's phases. *Ar
Hyd y Nos*. Insects intrude upon
those burying their medallions.

Those in the breadline await a
generous roll. Forgive the turkey
her blemishes as you carve her breast.

Undeterred by what occurred, homesteaders
flock to the volcano. Vigilant but not aggressive,
a man might keep to himself his shift in point
of view. One afterlife isn't sufficient to reward
everyone who has suffered.

## To Hear And Obey

This intangible currency generates its
own emotion. Even a man with no
poultry can purchase dry goods, free
from reprisal. Perched in a position of
neutrality, the stars are fixed in their courses.

The addition of Heliconia, and a tray of
soft olives, does not a successful soiree
make. A rendezvous implies you've met
more than once. A roundelay suggests the
song is cyclical. The booze doesn't make you
a better performer, it causes you to care
less about the performance.

You can only be eloquent in a man's own
language. The mountains beget clouds. A
mysterious allusion to *Mrs. White's Nothing*.
Buds burst forth on ornamentals. Reward
the horse that's never carried the caisson.

## From The Common Loon To The Varied Thrush

The luxuries afforded the acacia, with
respect to resurrection, may not be
extended to those who lay in its shade.

Some would rather lay blame on invisible
assailants than own their part in the
suffering of others.

It behooves us to put forth a positive
energy, to stand inside the lighted archway
until darkness descends.

Make the brightwork shine and receive
a sack of fern seed. Phenology not
Phrenology; when the bluebells will bloom
again, not what the bumps on your head mean.

The river may acquiesce to our whims,
but it will never submit to our will. Draw
no comfort from hindsight. Adam was made
to stand a thousand years on one foot as
penance for losing the garden.

# The Hand Of Glory

A day for apple-squires and shadow
traders, doves have chosen their mates,
daffodils have opened under oaks. A
bird lurks inside every egg. Place a piece
of straw from Death's effigy in the hen's
nest to better the brood. Let the honeysuckle
rest on the fencerail. The sun warms the
sorrel with a deliberate calm. Wear a loose
robe and walk among the crocus.

A chandelier of that size should've crushed
dozens. Such is the miracle of Haydn's
music. The wolves, howling on the ridge,
are reminders the lamps are low on fuel.
Stick around and list the stars of astronomy.
On whose scale is the weight of knowledge
measured?

As those who gather camphor are careful
not to grind their salt too fine, leave the bones
in your curry if you want to catch the crocodile.
Leave a man lame with a coffin nail in his footprint.
Don't break the seals until everyone has eaten. Don't
scorch the birch syrup with an unsteady flame.

# The Great Mondard

In blindness the mind still recalls
the fiery plumage of a scarlet tanager.
The soul is still stirred. Beware of
those who distrust nature. Those
who question the motives behind the
Monarch butterfly's migration. Animals
now considered unclean were once sacred.
Allow horses back into the Arican grove.

It's been observed that a bull tied to a fig
tree bcomes gentle. The chelidonius,
taken from a swallow, makes madmen
amiable. Fair speech mollifies a savage
heart. The liqor of love will render a man's
speech indiscernible. Myriad sacrifices are
made so that seeds sewn will grow in Spring.
Perform your most private rituals on nights
when no stranger is expected. The stars may
incline but they do not enforce.

## His Eyes Were Delighed

Let the night noises speak directly
to you. The wisdom of those who
serve is seldom heard above the roar
at the carving station. Cranes are no
longer roasted at table, but banquet
guests still expect a certain amount
of suffering before they're sated.

Expect a death in the royal family
if the ash tree fails to yield a proper
crop of keys, if the assayer takes a
holiday. The blind do not blush at
such naked folly. The distiller's
hyssop is harvested for absinthe.

An unexpected ascension and the people
gather to rejoice. Burn a white candle
for those who refused to destroy their
sacred books. The ox that eats corn
off the altar is simply taking possession
of his own.

## Borne On Slender Wing

Grass covers the ground where grain
once grew. Fair in feather, pleasant in
taste, we say of the pheasant in the fallow
field. Winter's porridge is stirred clockwise
on the stove.

From viscount to earl, bailiff to mayor;
everyone wants their station raised. Let
no man's title dictate how you hear the
music of the spheres.

It's hard to define the power all around;
what keeps us from screaming at the chorus.
Some live in fear of the day they'll have to
take a stand. Sometimes it's easier to weep
for a stranger than a next of kin.

## Those Intriguing Nightshades

When in the market for a black hen,
price should be of little concern. With
a duet, you must first find the song, then
look for accompaniment. The potential
for great reward abounds.

A carcass will bleed when in the presence
of its murderer. A blood groove in your
ceremonial blade may be frowned upon by
a more fearful mage. The images that
emerge from a shewstone may be no
different than those in a cup of coffee.

Be respectful to the flowers we tell
time by. Look for the deerhorn cactus
that greets midsummer midnight. Wolfberry
bushes, friendly to those who know their leaves.

# Mystagogue

Leave us alone, but don't go too far
afield, we beseech those indifferent
spirits that neither love nor hate us.
They that dance on heaths and greens,
and are seen near mines rich in ore.

Sylvester's tomb foretells the deaths
of popes. A nun ate lettuce without grace
and became possessed. Never consume
the mad honey of rhododendron. Sprinkle
your anvil with sage before you shoe a horse.

Maps always remember where the treaure is
buried. The mind creates mosaics with even
the slightest fragments of thought. If the wind
changes direction and clouds rapidly collect, the
king has put on his conjouring cap.

## An Uncertain Trumpet

We need more parades. How
can you kill a man handing out
flowers? Move from the spell
down the path along the brook.
Live off brown bread and leeks
for a while. A great misfortune,
not living long enough to be sacrificed.

No one should pass a sick person
in silence. The General weeps more
for his wounded steed than his dying
soldiers. It is ill-advised to declare war
on the western wind.

Let this be the day the Vestal fire
is rekindled. Elks and butterflies,
the images perceived among the flames.
Clarity before the blackout. We do
not always dwell on the discernible
side of light.

## Sewn For Ceremony

Tear away the first frightening thoughts.
Those new to deciduous forests are easily
fooled by winter's apparitions.

Little remains of Simon Stylites' pillar,
though all recall his wounded serpent. A
woman's attitude towards snakes has much
bearing on the fertility of a region's soil.

To know when to irrigate a field is a gift passed
down. Commit this image to memory if not
the waves.

Doves will be terrorized by angrier birds. Never
shoot an animal that mates for life if you're not
willing to kill both.

Peace after the winds cease, when stock
is taken of the crops. Those who toil at
the picking labour invent melody. To harvest
is to make music.

As the feel of the knife affects the taste
of the meat, the shape of the moon decides
the time of the feast.

# The Refrain First

If someone owes you money, draw a circle
around them. Dirt from the burial site of
St. Thomas will cure a fever. Things you
learn from a life of travel.

He goes by more names than chicory, but
the locals call him Ralph. These people
rear fish with more care than their children.
Mind the rudder or meet the rock.

As in threshing, some strive to finish
first. Others focus on the endurance.
Stones in the pathway aren't always a hindrance.
Collect them for the cairn you'll need
to build. The labyrinth is thoroughly known.

If we stay behind the veil we'll starve.
The white dog passed near him and his wife
miscarried. Such trials would put fever in a nightingale.

Do not accept the free heat of resentment. Osage
Orange is an efficient wood. It burns hot and can
be made into a handsome spoon. The stove measures
time in cords. Contemplation is often confused
for idleness by those unable to be introspective.
What roots us to this soil remains a mystery.

## Throwing The Fool

The walls will dry in their time. Wake
before the rooster and light the day's first
candle. Locusts still abound in the withered fields.
Keep a remnant of the most abundant crop in the
pocket of your finest coat.

The scents of a new season are welcomed with
bells and sticks. The cattle gather and sit. A
new storm gathers on the river's far bank. We
rise to wind and water.

The olive tree dreams of the oil can. Umbrellas
are envious of kites. Speak gutturally in the face
of a gale. As man grows more enlightened, so do
the deities he imagines.

## The Secret Fire, Traveler's Ease

If whoring is the oldest profession,
holy man and baker must round out
the trifecta. Is it possible to believe
in a creator without believing in salvation?

Imagine what has been lost in the whale's song
now that our boats are no longer built of wood.
Secrets in the wheat, divulged to the reaper.
A leaf, as it relates to the branch.

If your stone is vulnerable, admire its color.
What name have astronomers on other planets
given Earth? The mountain leans. The climbers
think of loved ones. This is the season for replacing
the mattress' straw. Even tyrants nap. Saxify
the desire to surrender. Don't pledge a kingdom
until you've tallied the letters of the leader's name.

When the spirit world chooses to communicate,
it will do so in a language you can comprehend.
Something will glimmer on the horizon, just beyond
what you know. Wisdom manifest through faultless
vision. Every plot of land contains a spirit.

Divination, be it by the observance of air
or the entrails of warriors, has led to a
common conclusion. The world cannot live
at the level of its prophets. Raise no sand over
the river man. Let the marble wings of tombstone
angels bear the departed up to Elijah.

Open the windows, uncover the beds. Pray
for the repose of the dead and leave a basket
of almonds beside the hearth. Light the lamps
so the shades may find their way to the feast. Give
the goblet first to those who've witnessed the work
of an unseen hand.

# SUSPICIOUS MINDS

## Bright Cup, Burnished Fighter

A brief and jejune June tea
dance segues into evening's primrose-
scented spectacle. Drop the needle
on Strauss and cue the fireflies.
Livy tells us a society in decay
will cease regarding its cooks as slaves,
and will praise their service as an art.
Cancers have a temperament fit for the
kitchen. Only Geminis should read palms.
The culture's not been the same since hersey
& peacocks were introduced to these shores.
Columbus brought the first cucumber to Haiti.
The sensitive throngs you offended years ago
with bestial behavior have been offended by antics
much worse in the meantime. Do not regret your past,
nor wish to shut the door on it. The earliest idylls are full
of uncorrupted & fragrant corpses. Pray you're
neither carried away in your sleep nor pierced
with iron. The finality inflicted by man without
thought; throw a stone in the ocean and know
it will never see the sun again. Aurora waits beside
the gate of Heaven for Helios to return
from his chariot ride across the skies.

# Ornithomancy

It may be false, this elegy I've composed
to honor the memory of warmth.

If we include wine with our afternoon meal,
the mountains won't seem so menacing.
We can linger and disappear.

I have found the stones that change their names
at dusk. I have been read to from the book
of forgotten shipwrecks.

I have studied the flight patterns of birds
renowned for their pitiable endurance. I am
determined to learn the direction of their migration.

## Perdita Peregrination

Proceed to the next tone
when you know what it should be.
We exist in a void, but it's a positive space.
We explored hard & deserve sponge baths.
Fish & think deep. Put salt in the dugout.
Poise in the pocket, poison the well.
Let the longest key point the way.
Easy to envy another man's acreage,
his hurrying bird. The newest eagle,
fresh down the stretch. I am a sunflower.
He loves Humanity, but doesn't give a
shit about people. He eats a bell
pepper & the strings crescendo.
A daring experiment, to say the least.
This is our sanctuary, frolic upon the upholstery.
Rain in the midlands, strong & weak fire.
Come through & make it right. Born to the purple,
the meaning is inexhaustible. A fragrant quiet fronts the sun.

## Special Rider

Home, how deep a spell
that word contains. Slow grows
the day when you've built upon
stone. Foresight and caution
have led us here.

If music is prophecy,
a study of harmony in numbers
should tell us what notes
the dawn holds in store.

As the acorn denotes poverty,
to dream of sparrows indicates
covetous neighbours.

And so the juggler raises
his left hand. Harlequin is Har.

How far this candle has shown the beams.

## Commodious Harbor In An UnHealthy Climate

Let's recap what we've learned.
The trees are down in all different
directions. This indicates a tornado
rather than straight line winds. Act
now & get a second set of steak
knives and an extra flavor injector. Stay
out of it unless you have to get there.
It's good to stop before you know
where you're going. It's all different
on the way out, a lighter heavy than
we're used to. Rock salt, burlap, &
pie tins. It's either a craft project from
hell or a new list of items for which you
must show photo ID to purchase. I
call these floating frames because they're
not attached to the art. Suddenly you're
on a bridge, being chased by a hateful bull
& a babbling green grocer. Remember Vishnu's
footprint is still visible on Mount Abu.
I'm open to it, I just don't see it. A reflective
catchall. A jaundiced auctioneer would
welcome your closet overflow. Talk to
the union about throwing the hammer down.
In these parts, only thing that gets cured is bacon.

## Crawl Space

I've got this handcuff trick, I've
got this phantom pain ... here. We
can watch the snow and forget the braying
beasts, cold and open.

Do you trust me enough to fall
in a dark room? Do you
trust me enough to feed you?
I am Abraham; there is nothing
caught in the thicket.

Between darkness and darkness
I pray into a copper pot. I sharpen
stones and breed camellias; don't
touch the red one, I haven't named it yet.

## Greased For The Channel

Thirty in two ought ten
though feel older than Turkana
Boy. The bang stick has
decimated the secondary. All
anyone wants is a safe place
to get a hard-on. A war criminal
once said belief and seeing
are often wrong. A deceased
anthropologist expressed that
the world began without people,
& it will end that way. Synchronized
movement, sudden sound. Music
hidden in the cantata. Remotest
lightning in densest woods. The
recital was flawless, but the reception
had static. What name do you
give the garden when nothing grows?
A suite of brawls on the barren plain.

## Lads, Back On The Horse

As fog gives back the mountain,
I devise ways to measure the weight of fire.
As things come apart in the mist, I learn
to value the names of trees close to home.

I've taken up this position because it's easy
to defend. I can nurse my chicory and bourbon
and still tend to my seedlings.

It's good, during an unjust war, to find
someone to share bread with. But I've
gone hungry many mornings just to feed my birds.

I've picked up windblown newspapers and seen
pictures of the burnings. I've rooted around
in darkness to find a man who'd accept
my small gifts.

## All One Word

The Sioux say the blue man destroys
us with greed & deception. Don't be
ashamed of your visions. Don't waste
your gunpowder celebrating armistice.
Peace exists beyond pain. Half asleep
you hear the BBC reporter say something
about an Ethiopian elder, 95 years younger
than his new, sixth wife. Puzzlement is part
of the condition. You can't knit with a larding
needle. Divestment is the name of the game.
Trust the cat to know where the house is warmest.
All you can do is make yourself available. Adjust
your sail to catch what wind there is. Stare
at the wall until you see the rooster. The owl
makes its home in all territories. Where the meadow
meets the timberline, it's impossible to see all
the creatures. The rustle of leaves gives their location away.

# Co. Aytch

Before the maps catch fire, before
the peculiar indictments are levied, let's
take water to the prisoners who make shoes
from sand. Let's pour libations for the inventors
who color our passions.

Before the horses bed for the ten-year night, before
a ban is placed on new flowers, before
the army begins its new-found war, let's
shave the geography of malice, and plant vegetables
that will grow beneath the surface of suspicion.

Before the official knocks on our door, before
I am given a weapon and asked to smite you,
let's dance to music we create deep in our throats.
Let's pull the blinds and dance, dance
with knives in our teeth.

# Early Snowball

I'd be lying if I said we
could go back to that. You
in your costume from *Gianni
Schicchi*, me clean-shaven and full
of bravado. The façade of order
requires a retinue to maintain.
The more moving parts, the more
to go wrong. The Japanese maple
has moved from mauve to crimson.
The brushwork is unorthodox, colors
bold. Baroque pop in the bedroom,
and Maria Merian's *Insects of Surinam*
in the antechamber. It's natural
to plan more than one narrative
at the outset of the day. There's
more than one way to kill a duck;
behead the Nantes, smother a Rouen.

## Do This To Remove The Necessity

I've been monitoring this frenzy
several hours now. Watch the blue one,
movements just beneath the shadows.

In the drawn and quartered afternoon,
we take comfort in our unknowing.
My thoughts of the sun mean little to those
who've begun the knitting process.

We will be travelling into new mountains,
into a new alphabet. We must pray
special prayers into our coats.

It's hard, even in the low notes,
to get free from such naked purpose.

Let's touch the far end of our sound
and reach into the new dimension.

The summers we spent clothed were meaningless.

## Armor Of Water

When music was young, elephants
were driven over cliffs, poets induced
to scream, burned alive inside bronze
bulls. There has always been violence
in the sublime.

A thousand sparrows have gathered and wept
on the site where I am to die. There will never
be enough spruce or willow to make the cellos
for my requiem.

Some believe a name with non-human
connotations will prevent Death from finding
you. Put me in a wagon bound for water.
Call me by the tree of my birth month.

Throw open the new screams and breed
flowers bright enough to keep our dreams
away. Sky is simply the space between birds.

# SOLOMON'S SEAL

# The October Horse

We've crossed the Blue Ridge divide and can
whisper our thoughts, at their first birth, to
trees unused to our native tongue. A clean
shave and a tumbler of spirits. The corn spirit
lurks in the guise of a hare. The trick is to do
as little as possible, but quitting will kill you.

Fasten purslane around your bed as protection
against magic. Purslane will fasten your loose
teeth. Our neighbor told us of an owl, which
caused a power disruption, and was roasted. Less
meat than a muscovy was the declaration. Destined
to lead apes into hell was the appraisal of the old maid.

Linden-scented soap and the lowing of a cow in the
coppice beyond the cottage. It's foolish to rob the
last house on a dead-end lane. It's either Blackbird
or Goat Island, depending on whose pastry you're tasting.
One sign marks a Cherokee victory, another a defeat.

## Promise Of Noon

Forced to rely on faith that autumn's foliage
exists, low moon over the Nantahala range. Check
the onion's skin to know what winter holds in store.
Turned green by duckweed, far away snakes the
Tallahatchie, rock of waters.

In a greenhouse made of glass plate negatives,
drinking brandy smuggled on horseback, it was
assessed the peak was upon us, Poseidon discovered
chickpeas, the Opimian vintage of 121 BC was still
spoken of with reverence seventy-nine years after
the birth of Christ.

Only a fool would choose a radish over a herring.
Lit in the garden, falling in the eggplant. Corn ripens
as much by night as by day. Darker than the inside of
a wolf's mouth. A swift witness wouldn't try to coax
fire through concrete.

A disgruntled initiate will don a papier-mâché helmet
and confuse a symbol with reality. If your characters
don't vacillate you have no play.

## Sacred But Fatal

Cool summer morning, waysides
starred with daisies, wayfarers
ever mindful of Adam Bell's name.
Jupiter's Beard will ward off a tempest.
The olives are safe under Minerva.

Consult the Book of St. Albans if
your hawk is ill. Hold the blooms
of vervain up to the fire for a vision
of the future. In a frenzy, the devoted will
unman themselves while women bake bread.

To offer fennel is to flatter, but
basil is a sign of devotion. It's our
misfortune to have been conceived. But
since we're here, let's enjoy the green
figs born of a twice-bearing tree.

## As A Swarm Of Bees To A Brass Pan

Agnostic as to an afterlife, past wrongs
and fitful triumphs kept alive in oral history.
Stretch out on a rocky crag shielded by scycamores
and turn your thoughts to Coleridge, convulsing
in opium withdrawal.

Days spent with the tipsy ballerina who'll
twirl to any tune. Practicing sympathetic
magic and waiting on the post for word of
St. Germain, aged 538 by popular account,
and last seen in Carroll Gardens.

Anoint the offending axe with fragrant oil.
A fresh fly will find birthroot a worthy
substitute for the carrion flower. There's
no sport in catching the goat if you own
the field. It's impossbile to be productive
in a house that's not been properly named.

## All Saints

The artist's vision would never hold the wall
were it not for the framer, who seldom realizes
fame. "Reality is the child of man's imagination,"
wrote a famous Hungarian with a brain tumor.
One autumn morning you notice a horse made
of glass on a plot of ground you pass with frequent
steps. What else has escaped your attention?

In some corner of time Simon the Magician is still
levitating in front of and above Simon Peter. Your
journeys needn't keep within the compass of reason.
Your labor is useless without the proper prayer at a
propitious moment.

Nature rewards the one who speaks her language.
Buddha's Hand, the arborist's delight, is fragrant
yet inedible. Smooth your bed upon rising, lest
someone take possession of your imprint.
If there's a spell to ease vexation cast it now.

## Acknowledge The Corn

Resident celibates, and those of the feminine
gland, fear not the frotteur, waiting for the parade.
It's not a feel to worry on. There is a tree in Costa
Rica that has leaves with waxy fingerprints.

Like a Turk pouring your gin, or owning a three-
legged sled dog, a day for picking clover is all
this is. The barometer indicates a sneeze in the
parlor. A feline in the attic, in the recumbent position.

Tell again the dream of Bedouins and falcons. Who
chased off Napoleon's little friend? Jonas Henry was
the first man in England to carry an umbrella. What
a figure he must have cut.

## Movement In The White Mist

Truth be known, if the food supply
dwindled to shoestrings, noblemen
would stoop to pick potatoes. Remember
the feast of sparrows in Constantinople.
Eat your brie with the confidence of Charlemagne.

If you come across a March Hare, give it a nickname,
in thoughtful silence, before you shoot it. The Aztec
prized the fur of the ocelot, though many preferred the margay.

Without the cape and coal you cannot cross the threshold.
Motley garments of a treacherous jester.

Pick the lock early. The first motions of the fiery heavens.
A universal excitement. Ask the crocodile why he loves the sandpiper.

# Shadow Light

At the Meeting of the Stones the bones of a
criminal would be crushed and a feast would
ensue. My bones ache with a knowning at the
beginning of Fall, and before a rain.

Some myths begin with the theft of fire, or a hunter
on the trail of a wounded deer. We're separated by
degrees of illumination and the shape of our vowels.

Trust a palfrey to be gentle, a diligent songbird
to lead you to sour cherries. Comets disappear
as quickly as cats in the presence of coyotes.

How a piece of music burrows a sense of place
in the mind. To hear a familiar melody in a foreign
outpost. The philanthropist gives a concert hall
to the rual community because he loves the local flora.

This system is not perfect, but the flaws are integral
to the work. Cold water aids a wound by tightening the skin,
but warmth is more soothing.

# The Whispering Campaign

Rule sixty-two reminds us we shouldn't
take ourselves too seriously. St. Hilarion
shunned the circus but tamed a Bactrian camel.

In our hearts we should hold out pity
for both cattle and kings; the terrified,
drunk and distracted.

Is it not enough to have sense and motion?
To be healed by the same hand that first
inflicted the wound.

Choose which form of liberation you can
live with. What is to be practiced and what
is to be put aside.

Plant your garden away from black walnuts
and build your home within a fence of safety
and peace.

## Carry The Bell Away

Long faces around the ballroom. The spoilers of countries, absurd in carriage and apparel, have been deposed.

Sailings ships have ceased their transport for the season. Serenity heralds the displacement of fear.

Hope is renewed with this transference of power.
Ivy embraces oak. The woodsplitter cleaves to his wedge.

Black bears have bed for winter. Graceful flight of geese on the wing.

The snow's not to blame for the trap it conceals.

What is the greater evil, to inflict pain or to kill in a single swoop?

If the fire requires more fuel, mark your page in the book with a costmary leaf.

Who cares what the key is made of, so long as it unlocks the library.

# WANHOPE

 IV

## All Joining Joyous And Mournful

There is purpose in each leaf
of the beech tree. Were it not
for pain, there'd be no
regard for the living.

Stare through your bourbon
and state the true color of the stars.
If you miss the train you can always
ride a horse.

As the worm moon approaches
we wake with more light
on the walls, and the glory
of birdsong.

Spring is always a race
between man and bird.
The lamp casts a different
glow with each lighting.

## That's Not Peru

This diamond is of the first
water. A faultfinder should perish.
The titmouse is a liar, but the
chickadee tells the truth.

A dog wouldn't even lick butter
off his forehead. He's deaf as
a white cat, but the cricket tea
made him a terrific singer.

Remember when we could sing
any song? Put a potato in the ground,
get a potato. Check it out and lock it
in. You could hold up a pot and catch
bullets. All the rivers around here are
named after death. There's a wound-
healing river known only to the hunted.

Great cry and little wool, as the Devil
when he sheared the hog. Cut neither hair
nor nails at sea. Curse all men of the sea.
When you're born to hang you'll never drown.

A preacher will tell you he'll take you
to heaven, but he'll take your money too.
15 cents will get you a meatball, but no bread.
We'll sup together after our dispute.

Don't buy your meat where you bury your
money. Don't get fooled by a different colored
ball. Some men would climb a tree to tell
a lie, when they could stand on the ground
and speak truth.

Children raised by wolves will howl. Black dogs don't believe in sin. The terror we heard in the forest was only falling acorns.

## Commisary Safe

Let's just say he got there. Someone knows.
It's getting dark around the edges. And before
we sit down to eat, to boot.

An iridescent bird. A new fish. Join in
a circle in the time between daybreak and day.
There are smells and sounds most people
will never know.

A splash, a dying ripple. Look, fresh mud.
And a small dog named after a vegetable.
Where can we be?

Futile to reckon how the finches have stolen
our grain. They will soon bother themselves
in the basil. Don't criticize the farmer. His hat
was made from eight different pieces of tweed.

## Spreading Without Let Or Hindrance

This is a mediocre year
for our cloud-covered planet.
The azaleas are pale. Parsnips
and pomegranates lie about, here and there.
Even if the singer is ignorant of the
source, the sourwood bends gently
in its breeze.

A book was discovered with the notation
of birdsong. But those birds live in another
province. The despair of the sparrow. Alive,
you're a spell against wicked magic. Dead,
you'll make the most delicious music.

This can only lead to blue ruin. Where
are the fabrics that will resist knives?
Cloth visible in everything. Shake glad
hands and remember the solemn days in
the mountains, developing a language that would die
with us.

Homeless deities. And no one knows
the name of Arion's dolphin. Half
an orange tastes as sweet as the whole.

You live in a meadow that does not
belong to you. Take off your clothes
and return it. Let silence close the folding
doors of speech. Let no man despise
the five finger grass.

What do you know of the one they call
The Ruination and The Light? We are
poor people, our nourishment comes from stone.
These stones will serve you. When work is finished,
lie drowsy in the hostas. You should see winter
on the line. A hare won't need spurs when the chase arrives.

Recall the stubborn staff in the moss.
Who devised chain? There's been movement
on the water. Claps in the wilderness, yet no
one will take heed. No one will run for crying.
If there is rest after this, can we sit down? The
sun will dry up the sea. Pharoah surely drowned.

Take the sickle away from Saturn and build
back up our dead dragon. Let us pass through
the earthly vale of tears. The wolf has devoured
the king. Throw the wolf in the river.

With gold the sky was split, and a fertile rain
fell upon the ground. Our dew is celestial and
electric. Let the moon kill his younger brothers.

## Between The House And The Holly Tree

Go make water in a shallow bowl and throw
it over the fire. Don't crowd out the pan with too
many mushrooms. If a lame deer stumbles
down from the mountain, feed it pears.

The crocuses are coming into view. Nature
is not visible, but it operates visibly. Drink,
drink for God's sake. The moon is on the move.

That man measures his cloth with an
unlawful yardstick. When shall we pace
again, tomorrow? This is not another Bible
and key conspiracy. Nothing convulsed.

No tongue for glory, small groups applaud
tyrants. What's worth more, a good book
or a true friend? In order to pray with more
conviction, some have been known to sell
their souls to Satan.

Our collecting days are over, now that we've
crossed our sevens. We construct our own small
worlds, and rejoice in their simple arrangement.

## Wanhope

To feel so much despair amid
this beauty is a curse. A laugh
over roasting meat, one stranger
with another. Joyous in the promise
of peaceful death; no more hovering
over cold fire.

Why won't this damn stone speak?

You can look at a newly sprouted pea
and imagine there is a creator behind
it. But all you find is dirt and water.

On the road to Ophir, gallant in deceitful
sunlight. Proof of a lost cause. The useless
thought of sitting for a portrait. No one
should know what we looked like.

# GOLDEN DAWN

## Jacquerie

No attempt at the picturesque,
another peasant revolt has left the orchard
bare. No amount of telekinesis can put
pears back on the branch. No pleasure
in restraint, to enjoy is to abuse.
To repine at what could not be helped.
Give a pearl to the man whose incantations
protect the divers. The image of the century's
first martyr is quickly capitalized upon.
*The phoenix does not appear, nor does*
*the river offer up its chart.* The fox is drawn out
of hiding, to investigate the violin sonata taking shape
in his woods. The siesta is a luxury free to the wealthy
& destitute alike. Dulled by the day's hunting,
larks in the graveyard provide a diversion. Gather
in the parlor for the mummy-unwrapping to start.
It's anyone's guess what we'll wind up with.

## The Question Is Lost

Wound-colored clouds
hover above the agapanthus.
Capricious spring morning
finds the robin wrestling
the earthworm.

An ill omen to find
buckshot in your oysters.

Lucifer lurks in the sulphur
of every match struck in vain.

Pour out a little new wine
in honor of he who first
trained the vine to the pole.

It's not yours to know
what the rustics do
amongst the corn.

Hold your coin until
you've smelled this potion.
This time the schism's
inevitable.

## Sorry Don't Feed The Bulldog

Be first at the finish line or a bullet
will find you there. Supper is served
at seven, as the freight lumbers by. A bountiful
board, complete with compote & tumblers.

        Bring out the asparagus, grown in beds
sewn with the sheep's horns. Eat a peck of
salt with the innkeeper before divulging
your identity. He knows Enochian &
wears a sleeveless reason. This language is
paper-thin, yet pliable; able to bear the weight
of fruit.

        Bear the thought of a winter
so cold, the wealthy burned books
in their chamber pots for warmth. These melting
memories are distractingly lighter than those
which have remained solid. Under the black flag,
a giving kitchen heals all woes.

        Fetch a Methuselah;
we've travelled the length of the Yangtze for this
soft turtle. These floors have seen a hundred years
of boot fashion. What we need is a breakfast of bacon
& fennel, in honor of St. Lucy. Bring your own fork.
"See whether raw or roasted I make the better meat,"

said St. Lawrence, broiled alive on the gridiron.
Soldiers, save my face, aim at my heart.

                                        Feel the flowers
growing. The most holy kind of fire has burned
the hundreth sacred Yew in this peacable kingdom.
Man can make gods by the dozen, but not a single worm.
I've left forests made wretched by our music.

## The Banishing Ritual

No honor among thieves, pillaging
epicures and prodigals alike. Nearly
a decade into a new century and high
seas piracy is still the most attractive
avocation around. But from this deciduous
forest, all we share with the Somali coast
are the stars. Studying Debrett's
etiquette alone in empty rooms will not
staunch the bloodshed in our world's
remote corners. If our old scholar
goes barefoot from his hermitage he's
gone back to the bottle. If he walks
out of these woods even the trees will
vanish in his wake. Pour your hopes for
a peaceful year into a bowl of fresh snow.
The wolf moon will soon be here to accept
your humble wishes.

## Transplanting Nymphaea

Bounced back from swine flu
only to injure his hamstring.
Such are the woes of the feckless
athlete. Too thin to get a tooth
in the second-hand quarry. A
wide stance & a look of freedom.
A safe ten is now a shaky three. No
painted clocks or checkered handkerchiefs.
Naked below the navel, with an upper
hand on wrath. Don't ash on the cheerleaders,
or throw dead rabbits at pregnant women.
Was a time a man could live in the Village
on pigeons & wild spinach. Spies
in all directions, just to keep the
middle clean. Test your ear on the natural
sounds. Mysterious as the stones of the
Racetrack Playa. By the time you've mastered
the optimist the mangoes will be ripe back home

## Cut From The Bolt This Secret

She is stubborn and the giver of life.
It does not matter where we aim our worship —
any fire or red stone will do.

Name the site where I am to wound you.
As ravens herald shades, we walk with trust
through new thickets.

On rain-weary plains we search
for new sounds. It takes great smoke
to shape such notes.

He is the slipping glimpser. A dull
knife is no more dangerous than
a handful of millet seed.

We can wave to the children,
but they'd better not ask for bread.
Now we find ourselves all alone,

in the trinket-giving season. You
needn't fear the night. It's worse
to see the beasts.

## A Sheaf Of Bearing Arrows

A whirlpool for the laureate, to
sooth his burning bones. A blooming
amaryllis and a jade egg. Across the
street the King of Sweden is selling Navajo
pottery. I know a man of parts whose
hobby is building steam engines. My dream
is to construct a ship of driftwood and paint
it green. Green is the color of courage.
By his own lights the mariner is guided.
Something happened to his hands so he became
a conductor. Some men can touch the magic,
and some men can Not. You can't eat potential.
We feast on wild honey, and feed our fire black
locust. Yes, you're on top. But what are you on
top of? Don't step on the portulaca. The unicorn's
in its pen, wild turkey beside the woodpile. A blue
haze hangs over the imbibitions.

## Split The Stick, You Will Find Me There

Oh, these afternoons bring on such fetishes.
We know the Devil has only one nostril, the
water spider brought us fire, aggression has
only one direction. Let's rivet together these
sounds and make one voice.

It's time to get on the forgiving line
and bear witness to the atrocities
caused by the wheel. Laymen and infidels
have lain hands on the edge of perception.

A hint of scale leads to false assumptions
and does little to comfort the children
who've been forced to murder their mothers.
To be orphaned is to possess a rare pearl.

What has been planted is to be rebuked.
Reach up with a natural hand and beat
the sun's daughter with sourwood rods.
The redbird is the daughter of the sun.

The blame lies on those too content
with the names of trees. We cannot
sit on this mountain drinking claret
forever. Most people are too blind to
even read the stars. The Pleiades and
the pine.

There are seven successive animations
before the final end. Turn and dance before
the seven trees. Retreat from adducing a plea.
The spiritis of the plants will tell you their uses.

## Day Is Done

Bite by bite and bit by bit we see
Galileo was correct. The way of sin
is broad but the crimp might find you
clean. You can tell from the outset
the ship will go down. Plover is in season
& certain rites are in the wings. A quail quill
can be more dangerous than a lion's claw.
What's become of the buckwheat cakes & cold
mutton, has the quiet man taken them away?
A dried grasshopper soaked in warm water
is a Xmas feast to your mocking bird. A meal
shared in peace is worth two in strife.
The voices of children must be a tonic
to the monarch. Let the bearing and the
barren duke it out. We need someone flamboyant
who can assemble a crib. Every night the lamp has oil
is cause for celebration. My, we've just seen
the flitterbick, and with our reputations, no
one will believe us. Drunk enough to break a pisspot
he stumbled then asked, what is the name
of the shin bone in your native tongue?
There exists a madness that causes a man to believe himself
an ox, boanthropy it's called. Those nights
when a lampshade worked as well as a derby.
The aim is to lunge forth, not to cut.
Sleeping with mint will impart wisdom;

a strike from the angelic hammer.
A long beard does not a philosopher make.
Why must the ignorant always discover
& defile our sacred spaces?
Does the moon rob the sun
of its light, or is it freely given? It's easy
to covet another man's walking stick.
How long shall ye tarry? Shake hands over a
dead mule and walk in opposite directions.
It's enough to share a vernal
pottage with lovers and friends. A feast
for the finer, invisible nature of man.
Truer of stone, delight in the sound
of your chisel. Wait in the dense forest
for the first tree to receive sunlight. Wait
for the water to be agitated by fire. This
is not the kind ferryman's shack. To
get there you must carve an oar.

# The Spirit Of The Staircase

Pave the way for tomorrow's walk.
If it's Thursday, we're having pickled
beets for supper. Keep up the breathing
and don't neglect the salad.

Don't be afraid if the chickens haven't
laid yet. Sometimes the door sticks. If
you want roasted possum, first you have
to catch a possum.

Some get sick off paint fumes, some off
pig farms. It's unbecoming to puke in
the hedge. It was lovely to have the chairs
recaned.

There was a request for nutmeg, but turmeric
could only be found. She's a real doxy, and
her addiction is well known. She goes by Mary
Frith, but we call her the Roaring Girl.

It takes years to become a Judicial Nipper.
Not just any conycatcher can make such a
boast. The tortoise knows a smooth language,
and makes a fine soup.

It seems all the best books need rebinding.
The windmill and the frying pan agree the
pine tree is an idol to the winsome.

If you want to be swept off your feet, hand
over the broom. It's easy to find a captive
audience on a stranded freighter.

It's a bad omen to die when the ground is frozen.
Never frequent a brothel that isn't painted white.
It's right to take pity on books the library no longer
wants.

Life is a strange avenue, with too many trees
for one man to know.

# Chimera

Man's symmetry owes much to the moon
& tides. Cast your glance upon the stony
shore. The delta's vines & branches are
supernal to the virgin eye, ignorant of their
predatory nature. How they strangle the native
trees. We have the peonies in their prime
all to ourselves until the new cottage
owner returns from abroad. Wrens repair
their nest in the eaves despite the weather
forecast. A year after karma claimed the
cat, rabbits are back. Half a century
of ornamental shrubbery cleared, the mason's
meticulous stonework exposed. The illusion
these stairs will always bear communicants
to the door. & what is communication but
the repeated rearrangement of a set of agreed
upon sounds. Will a humble gift of Golden
Delicious apples make the taciturn talkative?
Shoe a horse in silver & expect it to dance.
Consonant. Vowel. Conjunction. Vowel. Interjection.
The familiar shuffle, garland without ceremony.
Huntsmen dream of the elusive game. Addicts
dream of the elusive high. An indigo butning
appears once in the azaleas and is gone.

## A Rightness Of Its Own

Learn from those who can read in silence,
without moving their lips. Those who
praise the boat that delivers the morning's
sun. A glorious morning begins with the
sense you could easily ramble between the inner
& outer. As the ox is unconcerned with the money
it makes for its owner, we eat the bitter herbs
for the sweetness of their reward. We can blame
these shoddy apples on the decline of the Roman
Empire. No graceful flavor. Reach into the pantry
& fetch something delicious. Give away a jar of
preserves, but not the whole larder. By means
of death we preserve the beauty of certain species.
We save them for a higher purpose. Fresh rushes
on the floor, & the perfume of pomanders. Don't
stay too long in your grief. Don't stay too long at
the grave. Find the invisible nature as it manifests
itself in all things. The movement of its flight says
all the hawk needs to say. Strangers, resort &
speak to the wind's caprice. Like desperate birds
following the mast, some men move unceasingly
in hopes of grasping serenity. A change of scenery
will not suppress that stirring compulsion.

# Hell For Leather

How long it must have taken to comprehend
the silkworm and the mulberry leaf, that
basil and rue cannot abide one another,
the bond between truffle and oak, truffle
and lightning. Do not be fooled by the impatient
and ignorant among us who give no credence
to the license of time. Leave all the angles
to the defender. A long clearance, upside
and compsure. Fast in a small space. A
certain sound lends itself to this locale.
Nothing is hidden. There are no secrets,
nor is there control. That one's ability is natural
does not mean it's effortless. A man may display his
trophies but keep his killing tools out of view.
If the act of dying released a visible spirit,
imagine the high to be had in the witnessing.

## Inkeeper Grow The Pie

Bold as Beauchamp but
defensively indifferent. Effusive
to start, in turns avuncular.
Someone who knows the condition
firsthand would call you shitfaced.
A delicate soul would say you'd
been bitten by the barnmouse.
No more sounding your way through
Passamaquoddy in private quarters,
elucubrating into the night. Accuracy
is well within reach. Banana gas
just doesn't sound as lethal as even
mustard. The level at which
something benign will kill you.
Say woliwon when accepting seconds.
Be your palate for tallow or peppers,
may your tarry here pamper your tastes.

## Fireless Wine

Friends kidnapped by pirates, a near
fatal bite from a pit viper, the loneliness
of the sea. "Could we sail beneath a
redder sky," asked the captain, hoarse
and thirsty. The sea is a graveyard;
lift a glass to Hatteras Jack, who steered
every man to land.
                        If a man pulls down
the trident in the dark of night, he means
to do wrong. A skillet of bacon is a homemade
munitions factory. It's said albatross is a meat
favored aboard ships. Ships sleep with knowledge
of their sinking. When the bread is free, everyone
believes. Though we all toil at separate
labors, our bread is made from the same grain.
Make sure your baker is kind, lest you
eat from evil hands.
                      Afloat on broad water,
too restless to hold a rod. Trolling with
men who've tasted alligator and fear
neither whisky nor gunpowder. No more
guilt-free buzzes. By the time you're fully
aware of the sensation the experience is over.
A lethal piece of finishing.
                      Crown the man
king whose horse neighs first. Be it the sword

or the coin, no one in this world is spared.
Many with comfort but no glory, all too eager
for memories of the elephant they haven't seen.
Flood the reservoir with tales of our ancient family.
The Chaldeans believed a creature emerged from the sea
to teach the people to read and grow healing herbs.

    Those ignorant of fountains will never guess
the relationship between lions and water.

## Palingenesis

An attractive hearth, and the assurances afforded
by the *Popul Vuh*. What a thread of saffron offers
the broth. Wear a sprig of Artemisia on the Spring
Equinox. The towhee beds in the boxwood, shielded
from a mountain wind.

Familiar creak of a friend ascending the stair, to share
a meal. A brandy before the lighthouse begins its service.
Kind thoughts for those who steer by its science.

In the time when people still believed
storks hibernated underwater, on the beds
of rivers, how delicate the ferryman's job must have been.

The cover illustration is adapted from a frontispiece engraving in Joannis Agricola's *Commentariorum, Notarum, Observationum & Animadversionum in Johannis Poppii chymische Medicin, darinnen alle Process mit fleiss examinirt, von den Irrungen corrigirt, und mit etlich hundert newen Processen, geheimen Handgriffen, aus eigener Erfahrung vermehrt und illustrirt, Auch der rechte und warhafftige Gebrauch der Artzeneyen, mit etlich hundert Historien verificirt, Darneben was in Chirurgia und Alchimia oder transmutatione metallorum damit zu verrichten gründlichen offenbahret allen Standes-Personen, Medicis, Chirurgis, Chymicis, Balbirern, Feld-Scherern, Ross-ärtzten, Goldschmieden, und allen Haus-Wirthen hochnützlich zu lesen und zu gebrauchen* (Leipzig, 1638), and is used with the permission of Adam McLean.

www.ingramcontent.com/pod-product-compliance
Lightning Source LLC
Chambersburg PA
CBHW031207090426
42736CB00009B/816